Parental
Guidance
required

Parental
Guidance
required

ANDY STANLEY
& REGGIE JOINER

PARENTAL GUIDANCE REQUIRED STUDY GUIDE
published by Multnomah Publishers, Inc.

© 2004 by North Point Ministries, Inc.

International Standard Book Number: 1-59052-381-4

Cover design by David Carlson Design

Unless otherwise indicated, Scripture quotations are from:
The Holy Bible, New International Version
© 1973, 1984 by International Bible Society,
used by permission of Zondervan Publishing House
Multnomah is a trademark of Multnomah Publishers, Inc.,
and is registered in the U.S. Patent and Trademark Office.

The colophon is a trademark of Multnomah Publishers, Inc.
Printed in the United States of America

For information:
MULTNOMAH PUBLISHERS, INC.
POST OFFICE BOX 1720
SISTERS, OREGON 97759
05 06 07 08 09 10—10 9 8 7 6 5 4 3 2 1

[CONTENTS]

Parental Guidance Required by Andy Stanley
7

[1] Experience Isn't Everything
9

[2] The Three Dials
17

[3] Turning the Spiritual Dial in Your Child's Life
25

[4] The Big "I"
33

[5] Out of Control
41

[6] Turning the Relational Dial in Your Child's Life
49

Leader's Guide
57

[PARENTAL GUIDANCE REQUIRED]

by Andy Stanley

I want you to know up front that I've resisted teaching on the subject of parenting for many years. As a parent of grade-schoolers, I'm a little hesitant to speak with authority on an issue that I'm right in the middle of living myself—not to mention, a lot has been written and preached about parenting already.

But as a fellow parent, I can honestly say that Sandra and I cling to a handful of key principles every day in our parenting. And even though we're still works in progress ourselves, I am completely confident that you can also benefit from these principles.

Long before starting North Point Community Church, I worked in student ministry for many years. During that time, I saw many different parenting case studies lived out right in front of me. Some were examples of great parenting, and some were tragic mistakes. Through those experiences, I began to recognize several key principles at work in the relationships between parents and their children. Sandra and I quickly identified the models we wanted to follow and those we wanted to avoid. At the root of it all were these basic concepts about parenting. And in these next few weeks together, I'd like to share each one of them with you.

Of all the assignments God may give you throughout your time on this earth, none is more sacred than the task of raising your children. And while the culture around you may offer many suggestions about parenting, God has much to say about how to navigate the road ahead of you. I pray that God will give you clarity and insight as we study together so that you may be able to give your children the parental guidance that is required.

Andy Stanley

EXPERIENCE ISN'T EVERYTHING

[INTRODUCTION]

In our culture, parents can feel tremendous pressure
to give their kids the right "package" of experiences to
help them get ahead in life. We go to great lengths to
give them the best education available. But it doesn't
stop there. We arrange our schedules around a
myriad of practices, performances, games, and
gatherings—all in an effort to create the ultimate
experience for our children.

As society advances, the list of new activities
expands. Forty years ago, Little League baseball stood
unchallenged as the sport of choice for young
children. Today's parents must choose from soccer,
karate, hockey, gymnastics, swimming, lacrosse, and
other programs that offer advanced leagues with the
dream of Olympic gold and a jump-start on life.
Over the years, these programs have grown in their
sophistication and appeal.

To a large extent, we've come to believe that the key
to success is finding our child's niche in the right
combination of sports and/or art programs. There is

a tendency to think that forgoing an activity might mean depriving your child of the opportunity of a lifetime.

While childhood experiences are important, something else is even more important. As we'll discover in this session and in the weeks to come, an experience-rich childhood is no guarantee of a rich childhood.

[EXERCISE] Is Experience Truly the Best Teacher?

1. In column A below, list the various activities that you participated in as a child. In column B, list the key people who have impacted your life. Evaluate the importance of activities versus relationships in preparing you for adulthood. Share your thoughts with the group. Which column has had the greatest impact on you in your adulthood?

A	B
Childhood Activities:	Key Relationships:

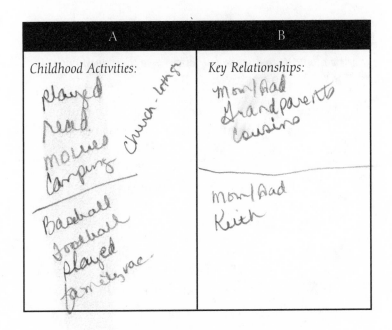

11

**"IT IS NOT WHAT A PERSON DOES,
BUT WHO HE IS, THAT GIVES HIM VALUE."**

[VIDEO NOTES]

From the video message, fill in the blanks.

1. The activities that use up our time and resources in childhood have very little to do with what happens to us in _____.

2. The trend in our culture is to make our children experience-_____ and relationship-_____.

[DISCUSSION QUESTIONS]

Take a few moments to discuss your answers to these questions with the group.

1. Why are parents today so prone to making their families experientially rich and relationally poor?

2. As you look back, how would you describe your childhood? Experientially or relationally rich or poor? Why?

3. What experiences have your children had that you never had? Is that important to you and why?

4. Where do you go for parenting advice?

5. As you and your spouse look at your parenting styles, who is more experiential and who is more relational?

13

6. If your children's experiences outweigh your time with them, what changes need to be made to reverse this trend?

[NOTES]

[MILEPOSTS] *Key Points*

☐ The pressure to participate in activities should not be allowed to govern your parenting to the point that it detracts from your ability to develop a strong relationship with your child.

☐ Children can grow up experience-poor and still thrive as adults, but children who grow up relationship-poor do not possess the emotional freedom to explore their life's full potential.

[WHAT WILL YOU DO?] *Assignment for the Week*

1. This week, observe your family's schedule. Approximately how many hours are dedicated to focused training in education, athletics, art, and other extracurricular activities?

2. Approximately how many hours are dedicated to focused relationship building—talking, playing games together, family activities, or just listening to each other?

15

[THINK ABOUT IT]

Read Luke 10:38–42. How does Martha's dilemma compare to your situation as a parent? What activities provide the greatest competition for the important relationships in your life?

[CHANGING YOUR MIND] *Scripture Memory*

The more familiar you are with God's ways,
the easier it will be to parent as He intended. There
are verses at the end of each session that we hope
you will take time to commit to memory.

> *The LORD does not look at the things man looks at. Man looks
> at the outward appearance, but the LORD looks at the heart.*
> 1 Samuel 16:7

SESSION

[2]

THE THREE DIALS

[INTRODUCTION]

As we've discovered already, the experiences we gain in childhood are not as important as the relationships that accompany them. Your child's experience in Little League may pave the way to a career as a professional athlete, but the intricate tapestry of relationships in his life will determine how well he manages his opportunities as an adult. Whether we play sports or take piano lessons, it's the people in our lives that have the deepest impact. In fact, the value of any experience in life is directly proportional to the value of the relationships we encounter as a result of that experience.

17

There are three specific types of relationships that determine how well a child is equipped to face life. Success in adulthood is largely determined by the quality and function of these three relationship types. If there is a deficit in any one of these areas during childhood, there is usually a corresponding deficiency in adulthood. Most people would agree that their greatest accomplishments and regrets in life were greatly impacted by the presence or absence of healthy activity in these three relationships.

During the fleeting window of time called parenthood, you have a unique opportunity to influence the quality of these three relationships in your child's life. In reality, no one else can provide the guidance your child needs in these areas like you, his parent. That's why experience is no substitute for your stewardship of the relationships in your child's life.

In this session, we will uncover these three crucial types of relationships and discuss how you can begin to dial them in and out of your child's life to prepare him to be all God intends him to be in adulthood.

18

[EXERCISE] Name That Relationship

1. In column A below, list your three greatest accomplishments or regrets in life. Beside each one in column B, list the relationships that were most influential in each experience. In column C, briefly describe how each relationship impacted your accomplishment or regret.

A Accomplishment/ Regret	B Key relationship(s)	C How impacted:
	parents friends	friends
	parents & in laws	Mother-in-law - supportive
	spouse parents in laws	very supportive caring & helpful - advice etc

19

"IT'S NOT WHAT YOU KNOW, BUT WHO YOU KNOW."

[VIDEO NOTES]

From the video message, fill in the blanks.

1. For the most part, our lives are the sum total of our relationships, our experiences, and our _decisions_ .

2. Your key _relationships_ have impacted your life more than anything else.

3. The three most important relationships in a person's life are his relationship with his parents, his relationship with _God_, and his relationships with people outside the home.

4. As parents, we can control neither the decisions our children will make nor all their experiences. But we have the ability to influence their key _relationships_ along the way.

[DISCUSSION QUESTIONS]

Take a few moments to discuss your answers to these questions with the group.

1. Do you agree that most of your experiences are related to your relationships?

2. Do you think many of your choices are based on what you learned or didn't learn from these relationships?

3. As you think back on your childhood, what was the setting on the three different relational dials?

4. Do you look back on your relationship with your parents with regret or relief?

5. Looking back to your childhood, are there people you regret meeting? Are there people you wish you met sooner?

6. How did the three relationships shape you? How are they shaping your children?

7. In what ways are you intentionally working to enhance your relationship with your children?

[NOTES]

[MILEPOSTS] *Key Points*

☐ There are three specific types of relationships—God, parents, and those outside the home—that determine how well a child is equipped to face life.

☐ As parents, we have a window of opportunity to impact the quality of these relationships in our child's life.

[WHAT WILL YOU DO?] *Assignment for the Week*

This week, observe the various relationships in your child's life. On a scale of 1–10 (10 being strongest), where is the dial currently set for each of the three key types of relationships?

1. Child's relationship with God:

2. Child's relationship with parents:

3. Child's relationship with others outside the home:

[THINK ABOUT IT]

Scripture commands parents to train their children. In the space below, list some specific ways you can begin to influence the key relationships in your child's life.

1. Ways to influence my child's relationship with God:

2. Ways to influence my child's relationship with me as his parent:

3. Ways to influence my child's relationship with others outside the home:

[CHANGING YOUR MIND] *Scripture Memory*

Seeing your child's life from God's perspective comes easier when your mind is filled with His Word. Rehearse God's mindset by meditating on this session's verse throughout the week.

These commandments that I give you today are to be upon your hearts. Impress them on your children. Talk about them when you sit at home and when you walk along the road, when you lie down and when you get up.

Deuteronomy 6:6–7

We explored the impact you could have on a person's life if you could dial in or out certain relationships along the way. As a parent, part of your job description includes controlling the relationship dials in your child's life.

SESSION
[3]

TURNING THE SPIRITUAL DIAL IN YOUR CHILD'S LIFE

[INTRODUCTION]

There is a natural hierarchy that should determine our priorities in parenting. It begins with the idea that your child's relationships are more important than his experiences when it comes to shaping his adulthood. Next comes the suggestion that his relationship with God—or lack thereof—is the most important of those relationships. Finally, there's the reality that you—the parent—have more potential to impact the way your child understands God than anyone else.

25

That being the case, one of your primary responsibilities in parenting is to help your child cultivate a personal relationship with God. But how can you do that? It's one thing to provide food, clothing, and an education for the first two decades of his life. But can you really be effective in introducing your child to the Creator of the universe? You may feel like you don't know God very well yourself. How can you fulfill the responsibility of dialing God into your child's life? The good news is that you don't need a degree in theology to be the spiritual leader for your child. All you need to do is assume the responsibility God has given you. And that can be as simple as knowing the right questions to ask. In this session, we'll explore three questions you can ask yourself to begin turning the spiritual dial in your child's life.

[EXERCISE] Fast-Forward

Picture your child developing spiritually into the
man or woman you long for him or her to become.
What would that look like? What kind of person
would he be? What spiritual disciplines would be
incorporated into his life? How would he handle
trials and serve others? What would his prayer life be
like? How would he rely on Scripture? In the space
below, write a few sentences to describe your child's
spiritual life as you hope it will be in his adulthood.

27

"THE SOUL NEVER THINKS WITHOUT A PICTURE." Aristotle

[VIDEO NOTES]

From the video message, fill in the blanks.

Three questions to help you turn the spiritual dial in your children's lives:

1. What do I want them to _____?

2. Where are they _____?

3. How can I help them take the next _____?

[DISCUSSION QUESTIONS]

Take a few moments to discuss your answers to these questions with the group.

1. Do you agree that you are the primary influencer in the spiritual development of your children?

2. How did your parents influence your relationship with God?

3. What aspect of God's character did you see in your parents?

4. What do you want your children to become?

5. Where are they right now?

6. How can you help them take the next step?

[NOTES]

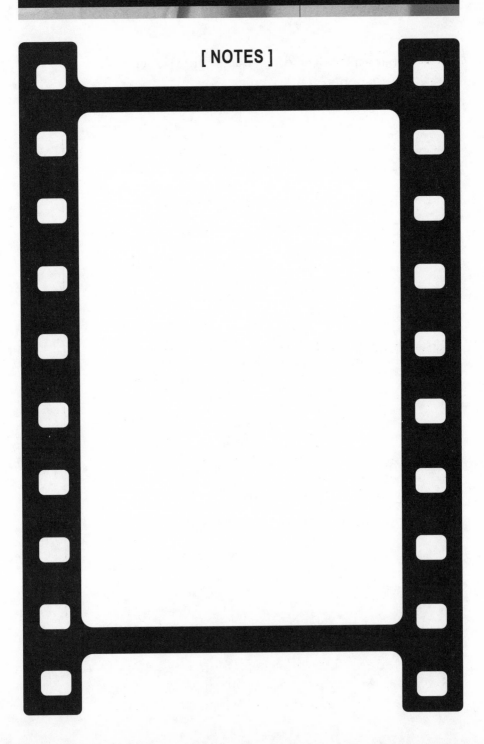

[MILEPOSTS] *Key Points*

☐ No one has more potential to affect the way a child sees God than his parents.

☐ Asking yourself these three questions will help you begin to turn the spiritual dial in your children's lives:

1. What do I want them to become?
2. Where are they now?
3. How can I help them take the next step?

[WHAT WILL YOU DO?] *Assignment for the Week*

Proverbs 3:5–6 outlines several core attributes that describe a person who holds a true picture of God. The first one is the word *trust*. In order to help your child gain an accurate knowledge of God, you must first make sure he understands the concept of trust. Thinking back on your own childhood, what was most influential in helping you develop a biblical understanding of trust?

31

[THINK ABOUT IT]

Trust is a vital concept. But the key events or practices that contributed to your growth may not have the same effect on your child. Bible memory, devotional habits, and Christian service are important disciplines for young children to learn, but each person is unique;

you never know which discipline will awaken an authentic desire for God in your child's heart. With your child's unique personality in mind, write down two or three ways you can help your child understand the concept of trust.

[CHANGING YOUR MIND] *Scripture Memory*

The authority of God's Word builds on the concept of trust. Train your mind to this principle by meditating on the verse for this week.

Trust in the LORD with all your heart and lean not on your own understanding; in all your ways acknowledge him, and he will make your paths straight.

Proverbs 3:5–6

[LAST WEEK...]

We learned that parents have more potential to impact the way a child sees God than any other person in his life. We also learned three key questions that can help you begin to turn the spiritual dial in your child's life.

SESSION

[4]

THE BiG "I"

[INTRODUCTION]

Your effectiveness as a parent is entirely dependent on your ability to maintain influence in your child's life. Influence is everything. In the early years, your size and position make it easy to exert influence over your child. You have the final say in virtually every decision in his life.

But somewhere between toddlerhood and the teenage years, a shift takes place. And if you don't also make a shift in your parenting methods, you may find yourself having lost the influence you need to parent your child effectively.

33

Our children need us the most during the critical decisions in their lives—decisions about school, career, dating, morality, and marriage. But sadly many parents find themselves with the least amount of influence during those crucial years. To make matters worse, their efforts to correct the problem often erode the relationship even further. It doesn't have to be that way. God has a plan to help you develop a rich, lasting relationship with your child that will enable you to be an invaluable influence during the defining moments in his life.

In this session, we'll explore the factors that determine the weight of your influence in your child's life. And you'll learn important strategies to help you maintain a position that will enable you to give your child the counsel he needs from you at the critical junctures ahead.

[EXERCISE] The Moment of Truth

Whether they know it or not, our children will need us most in the decisions that matter most. But by the time they're old enough to face those decisions, they're also old enough to choose whether or not they want our input. So how are you doing? If your child had to make an important decision today, would you be someone he truly depended on to help him? Be honest. In the space below, list the top five people you think your child would turn to if making an important life decision today.

1. _____

2. _____

3. _____

4. _____

5. _____

**"OUR CHILDREN WILL NEED US MOST
IN THE DECISIONS THAT MATTER MOST."**

[VIDEO NOTES]

From the video message, fill in the blanks.

1. When it matters most, the quality of your _____ with your children will determine the weight of your influence.

2. In the early years, a parent's influence is based on size and _____.

3. Your children need your influence the most when they make the _____ that matter the most.

[DISCUSSION QUESTIONS]

Take a few moments to discuss your answers to these questions with the group.

1. Why do parents tend to lead by size and position instead of by relationship?

2. How did your parents' influence affect your moral choices?

3. Did your parents or the parents of your friends ever try to "jump in late"? What was the outcome?

4. At what age should your children move from being parented by authority to being parented by influence?

5. How are you investing in your relationship with your children?

6. In what ways have you nurtured or nourished your children?

37

[MILEPOSTS] *Key Points*

☐ The quality of your relationship with your children will determine the weight of your influence.

☐ In the early years of parenting, influence is based on the parent's size and position.

[NOTES]

☐ Your children need your influence the most when they make the decisions that matter the most.

[WHAT WILL YOU DO?] *Assignment for the Week*

In the space below, write down the three most recent major decisions you've made. Beside each one, select the statement that most closely relates to your situation.

Decisions I Made	My Parents' Influence
	A. *I desired/sought my parents' advice* B. *I thought briefly about what my parents would say or do* C. *I didn't think to ask them* D. *They wouldn't have understood* E. *I didn't desire their opinion on the matter*
	A. *I desired/sought my parents' advice* B. *I thought briefly about what my parents would say or do* C. *I didn't think to ask them* D. *They wouldn't have understood* E. *I didn't desire their opinion on the matter*
	A. *I desired/sought my parents' advice* B. *I thought briefly about what my parents would say or do* C. *I didn't think to ask them* D. *They wouldn't have understood* E. *I didn't desire their opinion on the matter*

39

[THINK ABOUT IT]

In the situations you described above, how did your parents maintain or lose their influence on those decisions? Explain.

[CHANGING YOUR MIND] *Scripture Memory*

God is our heavenly Father, and we need His influence in our lives. One of the best ways to invite His influence is by memorizing His Word. Meditate on this session's verse throughout the week.

Train a child in the way he should go, and when he is old he will not turn from it.
Proverbs 22:6

We learned how to turn the dials that control your relationships with your children. Specifically, we examined ways to develop and maintain influence so that your child will value your input when it's time to make the decisions that matter most in his life.

SESSION

[5]

OUT OF CONTROL

[INTRODUCTION]

In the early stages of parenting, control is critical. The toddler years are enough to convince any parent that controlling your child is a prerequisite for raising him to adulthood. As a result, many parents draw the simplistic conclusion that if they can just control their children, then everything will work out. But in an effort to maintain control, many parents make a tragic mistake that undermines their effectiveness during the crucial later years.

In this session, we'll examine a familiar passage in Ephesians that reveals an important truth about parenting: There's more to raising a child than controlling him. And while control is essential in the beginning, it's only one stage in an important process. No matter how good you become at imposing your authority, there comes a point in parenting when authority isn't the goal anymore. In fact, if you fail to move out of the control phase at the appropriate time, much of what you do as a parent could have the opposite effect you intend.

41

Through Scripture, God points to the objectives parents need to embrace in each stage of parenting. And even when parents give up their control along the way, God never gives up His.

[EXERCISE] From Control to Influence

To practice recognizing the difference between parenting-by-control and parenting-by-influence, circle one word in column B to indicate which approach is the appropriate method for the corresponding situation in column A.

A (Situation)	B (Parenting Method)	
Selecting a pediatrician	Control	Influence
Completing homework	Control	Influence
Choosing a college to attend	Control	Influence
Choosing a spouse	Control	Influence

"HE WHO DEALS WITH AN OPEN HAND BEARS MORE INFLUENCE THAN ONE WHO RULES WITH A TIGHT GRIP."

43

[VIDEO NOTES]

From the video message, fill in the blanks.

1. To exasperate your child means to abuse your size or _____.

2. Your best bet for preparing your child for the future will be through _____ channels.

[DISCUSSION QUESTIONS]

Take a few moments to discuss your answers to these questions with the group.

1. How does a parent's relationship with his child impact the child's emotional well-being?

2. How did your relationship with your parents impact your other relationships?

3. What things did your parents prioritize over their relationship with you?

4. What are your children seeing in you that is impacting their relationships?

5. What are you doing to undermine your relationship with your child?

6. What needs to change in order for you to prioritize your relationships with your children?

45

[MILEPOSTS] *Key Points*

☐ To exasperate your child means to abuse your size or position.

☐ There comes a time in parenting when control is no longer the objective.

☐ Exasperation erodes relationships and destroys the leverage of influence.

[NOTES]

[WHAT WILL YOU DO?] *Assignment for the Week*

Read John 15:15. In this passage, how does Jesus demonstrate the transition from control to influence with His spiritual children?

[THINK ABOUT IT]

According to John 15:15b, what task did Jesus complete that marked the disciples' transition from servants to friends?

Using this example as a model for your parenting, what needs to take place in order for you to transition from control to influence?

47

[CHANGING YOUR MIND] *Scripture Memory*

God is the perfect parent, and His Word contains perfect advice for all parents. Memorize this session's verse to help you reflect His parenting style.

> *Fathers, do not exasperate your children; instead, bring*
> *them up in the training and instruction of the Lord.*
> Ephesians 6:4

We saw how easy it is for well-intentioned parents to exasperate their children, thus violating the warning of Ephesians 6:4. We also learned that while control is essential in the early years of parenting, it must soon be replaced by the objective of gaining influence through a healthy relationship with your child.

SESSION

[6]

TURNING THE RELATIONAL DIAL IN YOUR CHILD'S LIFE

[INTRODUCTION]

You may have the world's greatest relationship with your child. Your child may have a fantastic relationship with God. But there's one more dial in your child's life that has the power to change everything: friends.

It's a fact. Friends influence the quality and direction of our lives. Often the greatest successes and the biggest regrets of our lives are directly influenced by our friends. Startlingly, a friend has more potential to influence a person's decisions than either his parents or God.

49

It's easy for parents to overlook this category. We tend to think that friends are naturally drawn toward the people that are like them and away from those that are different. We think that friendships follow a natural progression and are therefore harmless. But you can—and should—influence the choices your child makes in the area of friendships.

In this session, we'll revisit a key passage from God's Word that gives very clear instruction and warning about the power of friendships. The relationships your child develops with people outside your home can be positive or negative. And it's the parent's job to be intentional in shaping these relationships.

[EXERCISE] Replacement Parts

In the exercise "Name That Relationship" in session 2, you listed your three greatest accomplishments or regrets in life and identified the relationships that were most influential in shaping those experiences. For this exercise, you will have the opportunity to go back in time and dial out the unwanted influences. In column A below, list your three or four greatest regrets in life. In column B, write the name of a friend you *wish* had been more influential in your life at that time.

A (Regret)	B (Replacement Friend)

"THE COMPANY WE KEEP IS LIKE THE SOUNDTRACK IN OUR LIVES...INEVITABLY WE WILL DANCE TO IT."

[VIDEO NOTES]

From the video message, fill in the blanks.

Start asking two questions consistently:

1. Is there someone you need to dial _____?

2. Is there someone you need to dial _____?

[DISCUSSION QUESTIONS]

Take a few moments to discuss your answers to these questions with the group.

1. Read Proverbs 13:20 again. How have you seen this principle played out?

2. What is one positive and one negative example of how your friends determined the direction and quality of your life?

3. Who is influencing your children now?

4. Are there people who need to be dialed in or out of your children's lives? How would you suggest doing this?

5. How are you investing in the relationships that will influence your children?

6. Are there other adults saying the same things you are saying?

53

[MILEPOSTS] *Key Points*

Friends influence the quality and direction of our lives.

Often the greatest successes and biggest regrets in our lives are directly influenced by our friends.

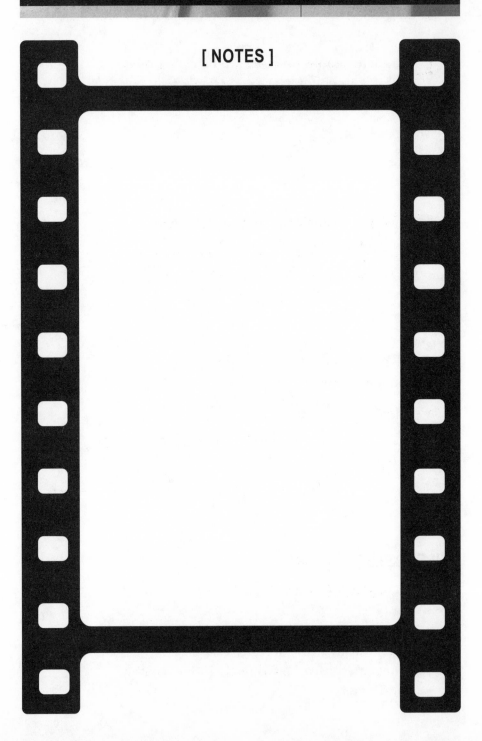

[NOTES]

☐ Parents should be active in dialing in good friendships and dialing out bad ones.

[WHAT WILL YOU DO?] *Assignment for the Week*

Read 1 Kings 12:6–11. How did Rehoboam's choice of friends affect his reaction to the wisdom offered by the elders who had served his father?

What does this passage suggest about the importance of influencing your child's friendships?

55

[THINK ABOUT IT]

Why are the opinions of friends often much more persuasive than the opinions of more reliable authorities?

[CHANGING YOUR MIND] *Scripture Memory*

God's principles flow naturally only when they become intrinsically linked with our everyday thinking. Meditating on Scripture is the best way to align your thinking with God's way of thinking.

> *He who walks with the wise grows wise, but a companion of fools suffers harm.*
>
> Proverbs 13:20

Parental
Guidance
required

[SO, YOU'RE THE LEADER...]

So you're the leader! Is that intimidating? Perhaps just exciting? No doubt you have some mental pictures of what it will look like, what you will say, and how it will go. Before you get too far into the planning process, there are some things you should know about leading a small-group discussion—some tried and true techniques. We've compiled them here to help you.

LEADING
[101]

BASICS ABOUT LEADING

1. **[DON'T TEACH...<u>FACILITATE</u>]** Perhaps you've been in a Sunday school class or Bible study in which the leader could answer any question and always had something interesting to say. It's easy to think you need to be like that, too. Relax. You don't. Leading a small group is quite different. Instead of being the featured act at the party, think of yourself as the host or hostess behind the scenes. Your primary job is to create an environment where people feel comfortable and to keep the meeting generally on track. Your party is most successful when your guests do most of the talking.

2. **[CULTIVATE DISCUSSION]** It's also easy to think that the meeting lives or dies by *your* ideas. In reality, the things that make a small-group meeting successful are the ideas of everyone in the group. The most valuable thing you can do is to get people to share their thoughts. That's how the relationships in your group will grow and thrive. Here's a rule: The impact of your study material will typically never exceed the impact of the relationships through which it was studied. The more meaningful the relationships, the more meaningful the study. In a sterile environment even the best material is suppressed.

3. **[POINT TO THE MATERIAL]** A good host or hostess gets the party going by offering delectable hors d'oeuvres and beverages. You too should be ready to serve up "delicacies" from the material. Sometimes you will simply read the discussion questions and invite everyone to respond. At

other times, you may encourage someone to share their own ideas. Remember, some of the best treats are the ones your guests will bring to the party. Go with the flow of the meeting, and be ready to pop out of the kitchen as needed.

4. **[DEPART FROM THE MATERIAL]** A talented ministry team has carefully designed this study for your small group. But that doesn't mean you should follow every part word for word. Knowing how and when to depart from the material is a valuable art. Nobody knows more about your people than you do. The narratives, questions, and exercises are here to provide a framework for discovery, however every group is motivated differently. Sometimes, the best way to start a small-group discussion is simply to ask, "Does anyone have any personal insights or revelations they'd like to share from this week's material?" Then sit back and listen.

5. **[STAY ON TRACK]** Conversation is like the currency of a small-group discussion. The more interchange, the healthier the "economy." However, you need to keep your objectives in mind. If your goal is to have a meaningful experience with this material, then you should make sure the discussion is contributing to that end. It's easy to get off on a tangent. Be prepared to interject politely and refocus the group. You may need to say something like, "Excuse me, we're obviously all interested in this subject; however, I just want to make sure we cover all the material for this week."

6. **[ABOVE ALL, PRAY]** The best communicators are the ones who manage to get out of God's way enough to let Him communicate *through* them. That's important to keep in mind. Books don't teach God's Word; neither do sermons or group discussions. God Himself speaks into the hearts of men and women, and prayer is our vital channel to communicate directly with Him. So cover your efforts in prayer. You don't just want God present at your meeting; you want Him to direct it.

We hope you find these suggestions helpful, and we hope you enjoy leading this study. You will find additional guides and suggestions for each session in the leader's guide notes that follow.

[LEADER'S GUIDE SESSION NOTES]

[SESSION 1] *EXPERIENCE ISN'T EVERYTHING*

KEY POINT:
In our culture, parents often feel pressured to give their children just the right "package" of experiences. As a result, many children grow up experience-rich and relationship-poor. The main point of this session is to present the case that relationships, not experiences, are the key to success in parenting.

EXERCISE:
The point of this exercise is to help people begin to see a connection between their past experiences and the people who played a role in shaping them. People tend to reference the landmarks in their lives by an experience or accomplishment, but arguably most of the significant developments can be traced to key people.

VIDEO NOTES:
1. The activities that use up our time and resources in childhood have very little to do with what happens to us in <u>adulthood</u>.
2. The trend in our culture is to make our children experience-<u>rich</u> and relationship-<u>poor</u>.

NOTES FOR DISCUSSION QUESTIONS:
1. Why are parents today so prone to making their families experientially rich and relationally poor?
   The purpose of this question is simply to get parents to engage on the issue of experience versus relationship. The actual answers are not as important as the thinking they require. This is an important first step that will lay the groundwork for more introspective questions later.

2. As you look back, how would you describe your childhood? Experientially or relationally rich or poor? Why?
   By reflecting on their own life experience, people in your group will better understand how this dynamic can impact a person's life.

61

3. What experiences have your children had that you never had? Is that important to you and why?
   There may be some significant improvements in the experiences from one generation to the next. However, no experience can substitute for the foundation that is achieved through a strong bond among family members.

4. Where do you go for parenting advice?
   It's important for parents to consider what voices around them impact their parenting. Taking an accurate inventory can be an eye-opening experience and can help motivate parents to be more intentional about where they turn for parenting philosophies.

5. As you and your spouse look at your parenting styles, who is more experiential and who is more relational?
   Considering each spouse's personality is another important element to understanding how a couple functions as a parental unit.

6. If your children's experiences outweigh your time with them, what changes need to be made to reverse this trend?
   Now is the time to start being strategic about how to parent differently. Encourage the people in your group to brainstorm some very practical ideas for monitoring and controlling the time spent with their children.

WHAT WILL YOU DO?
The goal of this assignment is to get parents to observe their family in action. Where are they spending their time? On experiences? Relationships? This assignment will help the parents in your group "take the lesson home" and begin to make connections between what is learned in class and how to apply it at home.

THINK ABOUT IT:
In this story, Jesus corrects Martha for being more concerned about experiences than relationships. This scene parallels the dynamics that a parent must navigate— knowing when to stop doing and start being.

[SESSION 2] *THE THREE DIALS*

KEY POINT:
This session introduces the key word picture for this series—the three dials. It is a metaphor to help parents visualize how relationships impact the course of our lives. Each of the dials represents one of the key relationship types: relationships with parents, relationship with God, and relationships with others outside the home. The more parents learn to "dial in" or "dial out" these influences in their child's life, the more successfully they can parent.

EXERCISE:
The point of this exercise is to help parents see the connection between the events in their lives and the relationships that shaped them. Who we know often determines what we do. If we examine the key turning points in our lives closely, we can begin to see how our quality of life is impacted by the company we keep.

VIDEO NOTES:
1. For the most part, our lives are the sum total of our relationships, our experiences, and our <u>decisions</u>.
2. Your key <u>relationships</u> have impacted your life more than anything else.
3. The three most important relationships in a person's life are his relationship with his parents, his relationship with <u>God</u>, and his relationships with people outside the home.
4. As parents, we can control neither the decisions our children will make nor all their experiences. But we have the ability to influence their key <u>relationships</u> along the way.

NOTES FOR DISCUSSION QUESTIONS:
1. Do you agree that most of your experiences are related to your relationships?
A good starting point is to discuss the basic notion that relationships impact our lives. This discussion will give participants the opportunity to embrace or reject that idea. In all likelihood, once they stop to consider its logic, they will ultimately conclude that it is true.

2. Do you think many of your choices are based on what you learned or didn't learn from these relationships?
   Obviously, all choices are the product of what we have learned or not learned. This question will give participants the opportunity to dig deeper into the cause-and-effect relationship between the people in their lives and the course of their lives.

3. As you think back on your childhood, what was the setting on the three different relational dials?
   You may want to suggest a scale for your group to use when expressing their answers (such as 1–10, or low to high). This question is designed to help parents examine each of the three relationship types in their own lives. When they do, it will be easier to see how these relationships impact their child's life as well.

4. Do you look back on your relationship with your parents with regret or relief?
   Digging deeper, these next two questions encourage participants to evaluate their past experiences in further detail. This question will raise awareness about the important role the parent-child relationship plays in developing their child's character.

5. Looking back to your childhood, are there people you regret meeting? Are there people you wish you had met sooner?
   This question will help parents begin visualizing the impact that can be achieved when these relationships are intentionally influenced by the parent.

6. How did the three relationships shape you? How are they shaping your children?
   This question brings the previous discussions to their ultimate conclusion. Use this time to reiterate that our relationships impact our lives—for children, just as they have for parents.

7. In what ways are you intentionally working to enhance your relationship with your children?
   For many parents, this may be a sobering question—they may be doing nothing to enhance this relationship. The main point is to help parents begin thinking of ways they can build a strong bond with their child. Try to get your group to share their ideas openly. The collective wisdom of the group can be a tremendous tool to equip parents for this challenge.

WHAT WILL YOU DO?

This assignment is one of the most important in this series. Parents must gain a clear understanding of the status of their child's relationships before they can influence them. Encourage your group to give this exercise ample thought and to be honest with themselves.

THINK ABOUT IT:

While this is also an important exercise, it can seem overwhelming. You may want to explain to participants that they don't have to come up with all the answers this week. The main goal is to begin to develop the habit of observing their child's relationships in terms of how they can be impacted. Remind them that the goal is not to control these relationships completely. They can still be successful parents by using minimal influence at strategic points in their child's life.

[SESSION 3] TURNING THE SPIRITUAL DIAL iN YOUR CHILD'S LIFE

KEY POINT:
One of the parent's primary responsibilities is to provide spiritual leadership. But that can be an overwhelming proposition. This session introduces three questions that can help parents provide effective spiritual leadership for their children.

EXERCISE:
The first step with any goal is to establish a very clear picture of the desired outcome. The more detailed, the better. Therefore, this is an extremely important exercise for parents. Encourage them to see the value of this exercise as a foundation for their parenting. The picture they develop during this activity will serve as a reference point both consciously and subconsciously throughout their remaining years as parents.

VIDEO NOTES:
1. What do I want them to <u>become</u>?
2. Where are they <u>now</u>?
3. How can I help them take the next <u>step</u>?

NOTES FOR DISCUSSION QUESTIONS:
1. Do you agree that you are the primary influencer in the spiritual development of your children?
   Try to encourage more than a yes or no answer to this question. It is important for parents to think about the responsibility they bear for their child's spiritual training. Unless they see that God intends them to direct this area in their child's life, they may never use all their resources as God desires.

2. How did your parents influence your relationship with God?
   When we contemplate how our parents have influenced our view of God, it's easier to see how we are influencing our children's view of God. This is a good question to help reveal important insights on this subject and is often very enjoyable for the participants to reflect and reminisce.

3. What aspect of God's character did you see in your parents?
   We draw much of our understanding of our heavenly Father's attributes from the role model of our earthly fathers and mothers. This question helps

parents to see the direct connection. It can be very motivational, encouraging participants to desire to model godly character for their children.

4. What do you want your children to become?
These answers can include any aspirations the parent holds for the child. However, try to encourage each person in the group to name at least one spiritual characteristic they want their child to model when he is grown.

5. Where are they right now?
Again, this session focuses on spiritual growth. Try to encourage parents to assess where their children are spiritually, not just in other areas.

6. How can you help them take the next step?
This is a brainstorming question. There are no right or wrong answers. It can be very helpful to get the group to generate many different ideas openly and share them with each other. Push each person to be able to name at least one very specific action step he can pursue in the coming week to help his child take the next step.

WHAT WILL YOU DO?
This exercise is intended to help parents reflect on what is required to cultivate trust. The goal is for parents to then identify ways they can parent to build trust in their child. The ultimate outcome is a child who understands how to trust in the Lord.

THINK ABOUT IT:
This exercise goes a step further, prompting the parent to name specific action steps that will build trust in his child. Make sure everyone leaves with at least one specific activity to pursue this week.

[SESSION 4] THE BIG "I"

KEY POINT:
The second relationship type this series examines is the parent's relationship with the child. As this session explores, the parent-child relationship is important because it determines the degree of influence the parent will have on the child's development. And without influence, parenting loses its effectiveness.

EXERCISE:
This exercise will help parents begin to think of all the places their child can turn for advice and direction. It may be sobering for some parents to consider that a time is coming when they might not be number one on the list. This realization can provide powerful motivation for parents to take action now to optimize their position of influence in the future.

VIDEO NOTES:
1. When it matters most, the quality of your <u>relationship</u> with your children will determine the weight of your influence.
2. In the early years, a parent's influence is based on size and <u>position</u>.
3. Your children need your influence the most when they make the <u>decisions</u> that matter the most.

NOTES FOR DISCUSSION QUESTIONS:
1. Why do parents tend to lead by size and position instead of by relationship?
The first step to long-term change is to uncover the motive behind the action. This question will help parents begin to understand some of the shortcuts they will be tempted to take unless they seek to lead by relationship instead of by size or position.

2. How did your parents' influence affect your moral choices?
Once again, parents can learn a lot about parenting by considering the way they were parented. Thinking back over our childhood, it's easy to imagine what techniques are effective in a child's life. Encourage your group to distinguish between what their parents did right and what they did wrong.

3. Did your parents or the parents of your friends ever try to "jump in late"? What was the outcome?
This question exposes one of the most common pitfalls in parenting. A few moments of reflection on some bad examples will provide additional motivation for parents to develop influence while they still have the opportunity.

4. At what age should your children move from being parented by authority to being parented by influence?
There are no right or wrong answers here. Obviously every child requires unique applications of parenting principles. However, it is important for parents to think about what strategies will work with their own children. This question will help them set specific age goals for developing a relationship that will allow them to parent by influence when the time comes.

5. How are you investing in your relationship with your children?
As a follow-up to the previous question, parents must also know specific things they can do to position themselves for optimal influence in the future. Now is the time. And this question pushes them to identify action steps that they can apply today. Encourage each person to name at least one specific thing they already do, or should be doing starting this week.

6. In what ways have you nurtured or nourished your children?
Invariably, every parent has already had some successes in this area. Encourage them by rehearsing what has worked. This will also give them a foundation to build on as they seek to cultivate the relationship further as they move toward adulthood.

WHAT WILL YOU DO?
The purpose of this exercise is to help parents develop a vision for how their children might seek their influence in the future. As the answers suggest, it's possible to develop such a strong relationship that children come back to you again and again for your input. Depending on their own experience growing up, the people in your group might never have imagined such possibilities. Now they can.

THINK ABOUT IT:
This follow-up exercise helps participants to identify the cause-and-effect relationships that determine whether parents keep influence or lose it.

[SESSION 5] *OUT OF CONTROL*

KEY POINT:
The goal of parenting is to move out of the control phase and into the influence phase. Of course, parenting requires that a parent establish control over the child in the early years, but parents who fail to relinquish control at the appropriate time and move to parenting-by-influence can destroy relationships and undermine their parenting.

EXERCISE:
This exercise will take the participant through several real-life scenarios in which parents practice either control or influence. For example, selecting a pediatrician is usually not an age-appropriate decision for a young child. Encouraging completion of homework depends on the age and personality of the child. Selecting a college can also depend on the child's maturity and level of assertiveness. Choosing a spouse may be influenced by the parent, but it is unlikely to be controlled.

VIDEO NOTES:
1. To exasperate your child means to abuse your size or <u>position</u>.
2. Your best bet for preparing your child for the future will be through <u>relational</u> channels.

NOTES FOR DISCUSSION QUESTIONS:
1. How does a parent's relationship with his child impact his child's emotional well-being?
    This is an excellent conversation starter for this session. It may expose diverse opinions about how parents impact their child's emotions. As the question implies, emotional well-being is a fundamental quality of a child who is able to make competent, age-appropriate decisions without requiring the parent to control every situation.

2. How did your relationship with your parents impact your other relationships?
    As this question suggests, the parent-child relationship causes a ripple effect that impacts the child's entire social structure. When parents review their own history, it underscores the importance of cultivating strong, healthy relationships with their children.

70

3. What things did your parents prioritize over their relationship with you?
By pondering this question, parents will be encouraged to consider the impact their own priorities and choices will have on their children. By reviewing their own experiences, they will be able to attach feelings to the subject.

4. What are your children seeing in you that is impacting their relationships?
This is an important question for parents. It is always a good idea to keep track of the qualities that are visible to our children. What they see is all they have to help them develop their worldview. It is also likely to be what they will model.

5. What are you doing to undermine your relationships with your children?
On a similar note, parents should look for any behavior or patterns that might be subtle, eroding factors in their relationships with their children. Try to encourage participants to share numerous examples. This will help uncover blind spots for other parents.

6. What needs to change in order for you to prioritize your relationships with your children?
Finally, encourage everyone in the group to identify at least one specific action he can take this week to ensure that the parent-child relationship is prioritized appropriately.

WHAT WILL YOU DO?
Jesus modeled the principle of leading-by-influence during His ministry. Though this passage is not specifically about parenting, it gives parents a vivid picture of what it looks like to turn over control to those who have been properly taught to manage it.

THINK ABOUT IT:
This passage lends valuable insight into parenting. As parents, we have a tendency to feel responsible for the outcome. This leads to an excessive desire for control. In reality, God is responsible for the outcome. Your responsibility ends once you have "made known," or transferred, to the child everything you have learned—including an understanding of God's love through Christ Jesus. Beyond that point, the role of the parent should be one of influence, not control.

[SESSION 6] TURNING THE RELATIONAL DIAL IN YOUR CHILD'S LIFE

KEY POINT:
Many parents overlook the tremendous power of influence that friends can have in a child's life. Parental guidance in this area is essential. God's Word is clear about the blessings—and consequences—of cultivating the right friendships. This session gives parents a practical understanding of their role in influencing their child's friendships.

EXERCISE:
This exercise will help parents begin to consider the influence friends have had in their lives. Understanding this dynamic will help them appreciate the importance of helping their children develop strategic friendships.

VIDEO NOTES:
1. Is there someone you need to dial <u>out</u>?
2. Is there someone you need to dial <u>in</u>?

NOTES FOR DISCUSSION QUESTIONS:
1. Read Proverbs 13:20 again. How have you seen this principle played out?
   This is an opportunity for you to initiate discussion about the influence of friendships. Without being judgmental, try to come up with some well-known examples of people whose decisions were enhanced or corrupted by those around them.

2. What is one positive and one negative example of how your friends determined the direction and quality of your life?
   This question will likely rekindle discussion of the previous exercise. Ask parents to suggest some ways their lives would be different had they chosen different friendships.

3. Who is influencing your children now?
   For parents of older children, this can be a sobering question. But make sure parents of younger children use their imaginations to fully embrace the time when their children's friends will play a pivotal role in determining their course in life.

4. Are there people who need to be dialed in or out of your children's lives? How would you suggest doing this?
Some parents might hesitate to pronounce judgment on their child's choice of friends. Others might be overly controlling. Encourage your group to accept their roles as influencers in this important area. At the same time, remind them that they must handle this responsibility with love and care.

5. How are you investing in the relationships that will influence your children?
It's a tough task, but parents can influence the outside relationships their children develop. It can require a lot of foresight and involvement. Around the group, share examples of steps parents can take to cultivate helpful relationships with others outside the home.

6. Are there other adults saying the same things you are saying?
One of the most important factors in shaping a young person's belief system is to hear his parents' values reaffirmed by an independent source he respects. It is important for parents to consider the environments they are encouraging for their children outside the home. With foresight, parents can increase the likelihood their values will be reinforced by other adults in their child's life.

WHAT WILL YOU DO?
This is a classic passage of a young person making decisions on his own. As you discuss this story, there may be numerous parallels drawn with your group's own experiences. You may ask parents to share how they would have parented Rehoboam to achieve a more desirable outcome.

THINK ABOUT IT:
There are no right or wrong answers. However, you may note that friends gain influence because we allow them access to our hearts. Time and exposure to friends eventually impacts our worldview—we tend to become like those around us. Unless we are firmly rooted in our belief system, we are vulnerable to dissuasion from it. No matter how reliable an authority figure, it is no match for the influences that receive free access to our time and our hearts.

73